First Facts®

EXTREME PLANET

THE DRIEST PLACES ON EARTH

by Martha E. H. Rustad

Consultant:
Randall S. Cerveny, PhD
President's Professor, School of Geographical Sciences
Arizona State University, Tempe

CAPSTONE PRESS
a capstone imprint

First Facts is published by Capstone Press,
151 Good Counsel Drive, P.O. Box 669, Mankato, Minnesota 56002.
www.capstonepress.com

092009
005618CGS10

Books published by Capstone Press are manufactured with paper
containing at least 10 percent post-consumer waste.

Library of Congress Cataloging-in-Publication Data
Rustad, Martha E. H. (Martha Elizabeth Hillman), 1975–
    The driest places on Earth / by Martha E. H. Rustad.
        p. cm. — (First facts. Extreme planet)
    Summary: "An introduction to the driest places on Earth, including maps and colorful
photographs" — Provided by publisher.
    Includes bibliographical references and index.
    ISBN 978-1-4296-3962-0 (library binding)
    1. Arid regions climate — Juvenile literature. 2. Climatic extremes — Juvenile literature. 3. Arid
regions — Description and travel — Juvenile literature. I. Title. II. Series.
QC993.7R87 2010
551.41'5 — dc22   2009026037

Editorial credits
Erika L. Shores, editor; Ted Williams, designer; Svetlana Zhurkin, media researcher;
    Eric Manske, production specialist

Photo credits
Alamy/Andrew McConnell, 19; RIA Novosti, 9; travelbild, 13
Getty Images/National Geographic/George F. Mobley, 16; Photographer's Choice/Maremagnum, 7;
    Quinn Rooney, 10
iStockphoto/Domenico Pellegriti, cover; Steve Geer, 21
Shutterstock/Dmitry Pichugin, 5; Holger Mette, 15

Essential content terms are **bold** and are defined at the bottom of the spread
where they first appear.

TABLE OF CONTENTS

Hot and Dry 4

DRY!
Mauna Kea Observatory 6
Astrakhan, Russia 8

DRIER!
Troudaninna, Australia 11
Aden, Yemen 12
Batagues, Mexico 14

DRIEST!
Amundsen-Scott South Pole Station 17
Wadi Halfa, Sudan 18
Arica, Chile 20

GLOSSARY 22
READ MORE 23
INTERNET SITES 23
INDEX 24

Hot and Dry

Imagine living in the driest place on earth. Is the air hot? Is the dirt hard and cracked under your feet? Is your mouth dry? People, animals, and plants need water to live. In places where little rain falls, life can be hard. Let's explore the driest places on each **continent**.

> **continent** — one of earth's seven large land masses

8 MAUNA KEA OBSERVATORY

Islands are usually wet places. But a spot on the island of Hawaii stays dry much of the year. An **observatory** sits high on a mountain named Mauna Kea. Clear, dry weather lets telescopes see far into space. Clouds rarely form over Mauna Kea. Each year, only about 7.41 inches (18.8 centimeters) of rain falls at the observatory.

observatory — a building with telescopes and other scientific instruments for studying the sky, stars, and planets

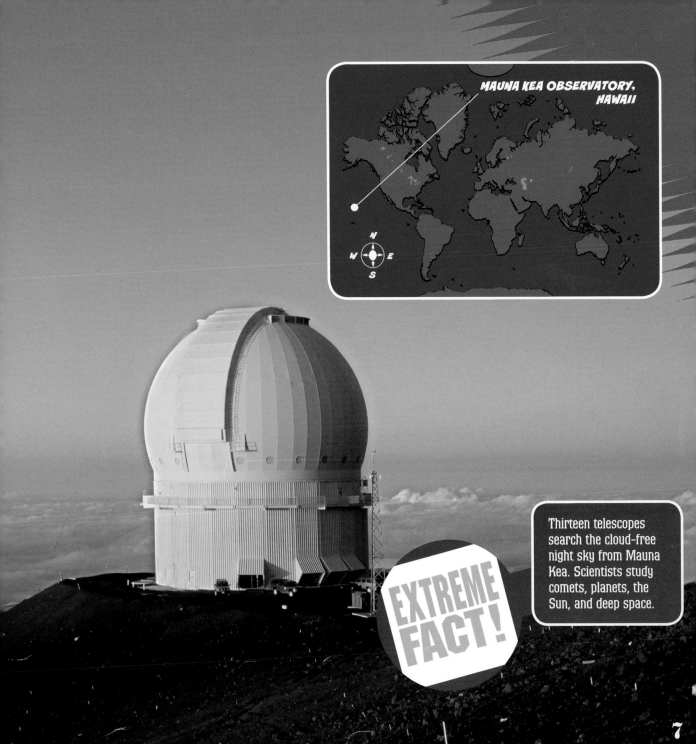

MAUNA KEA OBSERVATORY, HAWAII

W N E S

EXTREME FACT!

Thirteen telescopes search the cloud-free night sky from Mauna Kea. Scientists study comets, planets, the Sun, and deep space.

7 ASTRAKHAN, RUSSIA

Eleven islands make up the city of Astrakhan, Russia. This European city sits in the **arid** prairies around the Volga River. This area of grasslands is extremely dry. Each year, only around 6.4 inches (16.3 centimeters) of **precipitation** falls.

arid — dry
precipitation — water that falls from clouds to the earth's surface in the form of rain, hail, sleet, or snow

ASTRAKHAN, RUSSIA

TROUDANINNA, AUSTRALIA

N
W E
S

Birds fly as far as 1,200 miles (1,931 kilometers) to Lake Eyre when it's filled.

EXTREME FACT!

TROUDANINNA, AUSTRALIA

6

Troudaninna is the driest place in Australia. Only 4.05 inches (10.3 centimeters) of rain falls there each year. Troudaninna is near Lake Eyre. The lake is dry most of the time. But once every eight years enough rain falls to flood the lake. The flooding turns it into the biggest lake in Australia.

5 ADEN, YEMEN

Yemen is a hot, dry country in the Arabian **Desert**. In Aden, Yemen, only about 1.8 inches (4.6 centimeters) of rain falls yearly.

Although little rain falls, the air is humid. Hot air from the nearby Persian Gulf and Red Sea holds a lot of water vapor. It makes the air feel sticky and uncomfortable.

desert — an area where very little rain falls

ADEN, YEMEN

13

4 BATAGUES, MEXICO

Warm, wet air blows into the Baja California peninsula from the Pacific Ocean. The wet air drops heavy rainfall on mountains there.

After it rains, dry air is pushed eastward. Little rain falls on the peninsula's eastern side where Batagues, Mexico, is located. With 1.2 inches (3 centimeters) of rain yearly, it's North America's driest place.

BATAGUES, MEXICO

N W E S

EXTREME FACT!

Many types of cactuses grow in Batagues. These plants grow well in the dry, hot weather.

AMUNDSEN-SCOTT SOUTH
POLE STATION, ANTARCTICA

N
W E
S

UNITED STATES WELCOMES YOU
TO THE SOUTH POLE

During winter, about 50 people live
at the South Pole. In summer, about
150 people live there. They must
melt the ice to get drinking water.

EXTREME
FACT!

AMUNDSEN-SCOTT SOUTH POLE STATION

Antarctica is a cold desert. Each year, only about 0.8 inch (2 centimeters) of snow falls at Amundsen-Scott South Pole Station. The station is built on a sheet of ice about 9,000 feet (2,700 meters) thick. This ice is made of snow that never melts.

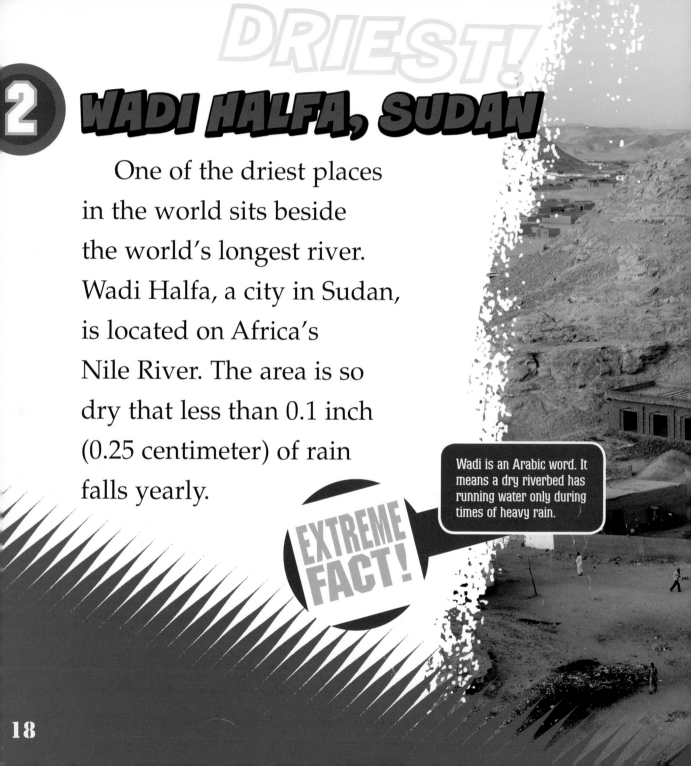

2 WADI HALFA, SUDAN

One of the driest places in the world sits beside the world's longest river. Wadi Halfa, a city in Sudan, is located on Africa's Nile River. The area is so dry that less than 0.1 inch (0.25 centimeter) of rain falls yearly.

EXTREME FACT!

Wadi is an Arabic word. It means a dry riverbed has running water only during times of heavy rain.

WADI HALFA, SUDAN

19

1 ARICA, CHILE

If you travel to Arica, Chile, in the Atacama Desert, leave your umbrella at home. Rain almost never falls. The city gets about 0.03 inch (0.08 centimeter) each year. But the air can be wet and sticky. Fog and dew form often. The humidity gives moisture to people, animals, and plants in Arica. They find ways to live in the driest place on earth.

ARICA, CHILE

GLOSSARY

arid (A-rid) — dry

continent (KAHN-tuh-nuhnt) — one of earth's seven large land masses

desert (DEZ-urt) — an area where very little rain falls

humidity (hyoo-MIH-du-tee) — the measure of the moisture in the air

observatory (uhb-ZUR-vuh-tor-ee) — a building with telescopes and other scientific instruments for studying the sky, stars, and planets

peninsula (puh-NIN-suh-luh) — a piece of land that is surrounded by water on three sides

precipitation (pri-sip-i-TAY-shuhn) — water that falls from clouds to the earth's surface in the form of rain, hail, sleet, or snow

READ MORE

Birch, Robin. *Earth's Climate.* Weather and Climate. New York: Marshall Cavendish Benchmark, 2009.

Greenberger, Robert. *Deserts: The Living Landscape.* Biomes of the World. New York: Rosen, 2009.

Morrison, Ian A. *Deserts of the World.* Our Planet. New York: PowerKids Press, 2009.

INTERNET SITES

FactHound offers a safe, fun way to find Internet sites related to this book. All of the sites on FactHound have been researched by our staff.

Here's all you do:

Visit *www.facthound.com*

FactHound will fetch the best sites for you!

INDEX

Aden, Yemen, 12
Amundsen-Scott South Pole
    Station, 16, 17
Antarctica, 17
Arabian Desert, 12
Arica, Chile, 20
Astrakhan, Russia, 8
Atacama Desert, 20

Baja California peninsula, 14
Batagues, Mexico, 14

Hawaii, 6
humidity, 12, 20

Lake Eyre, 10, 11

Mauna Kea Observatory, 6, 7
mountains, 6, 14

Nile River, 18

Pacific Ocean, 14
Persian Gulf, 12
prairies, 8

Red Sea, 12

Troudaninna, Australia, 11

Volga River, 8

Wadi Halfa, Sudan, 18